Mental Toughness:

The Ultimate Guide To Train Your Brain, Boost Your Resilience, Discover How To Be Relentless With True Mindset And Become Unbeatable With An Unstoppable Mind

indirect, which are incurred as a result of the use of information contained within this document, including, but not limited to, — errors, omissions, or inaccuracies.

Table of Contents

Introduction

Congratulations on purchasing *Mental Toughness: The Ultimate Guide To Train Your Brain, Boost Your Resilience, Discover How To Be Relentless With True Mindset And Become Unbeatable With An Unstoppable Mind* and thank you for doing so.

The following chapters will discuss how you can handle the various tough situations in your life and yet be mentally strong. Being mentally strong is something you need to master over time because it is not something that comes automatically. It will take you time and there is no need to beat yourself for the fact that you are too sensitive. Resiliency is something that everyone who wants to be successful in life has to master.

Do you feel that you are stuck somewhere in your life? Do you feel that your goals and aspirations are now a far-fetched dream just because you are facing some adversities? Then, this book is exactly what you need because here, you will learn about how you should be consistent at your work even if everything is going wrong around you. You will learn to work your way past the challenges in your life and make it big. You will also learn the importance of goal-setting and how to do it efficiently. And in between all of these things, you will be developing your leadership qualities by working on grooming an unbeatable mind.

There are plenty of books on this subject on the market, thanks again for choosing this one! Every effort was made to ensure it is full of as much useful information as possible, please enjoy!

Chapter 1

What Is Mental Toughness?

Mental toughness is the strength of the mind to fight against circumstantial pressures, stressors, and challenges in which you are staying. It is an exercise of the mental power to overcome the shortcomings that create problems to you without blaming others. Mental power exercise when practiced regularly helps you to perform better to a large extent against the prevailing difficulties and barriers. Today's hustle and bustle activities have indeed made life more complex and stressful. If you look 100 years back, you could see that people would live their lives in a poor habitable and dietary condition. They were unhappy but not stressed because they were mentally sound and strong. Today people feel more stressed than their ancestors due to lack of mental strength.

Key Components of Mental Toughness

Main characteristics of mental ability can be sub-divided into three components viz., emotion, behavior, and confidence. These three components play a key role to help you become a more resilient and self-driven person. Let's discuss the components one by one.

- **Emotion** – It is a state of mind that involves a feeling in a situation or relationship with other people. Your feelings in a situation involve almost all activities surrounding you. It extends from home to your workplace and even to your societal relationships. Similarly, the relationship with others involves a relationship with your family members and even your colleagues and friends. It also includes your neighbors. Without emotion, you cannot connect with the people or the situation.

Let's take an example. You have prepared a new project for your company in which you are emotionally involved. You have been asked to give a demo of the project before colleagues and higher officials. It can bring a new opportunity which can expand the company's business and profit. If the project becomes successful, the chances are that you will be promoted to a superior post. Here, emotion is your mental strength. Now, when you are demonstrating your project, few colleagues pass on negative remarks and opinions asking some questions. You strongly argue in favor of your project logically and at the same time, you ignore their questions and do not hear them with due respect. Being ignored by you, the colleagues and higher officials altogether can reject the project though it has a new possibility. Here, emotion is your mental weakness.

From the above example, it can be said when emotion is mental strength, it can create opportunity, but when it is a weakness it might hinder your success. Here, emotional weakness has greatly affected the professional attitude and opportunity of the new project is lost in all respect. So, you should control your emotion before emotion controls you and proactively express your emotion to the colleagues so that they can make the best choice.

So, to achieve a strong mental ability and resiliency to overcome the weakness and eliminate any threat to your growth, you have to exercise and achieve the followings three skills:

1. Apply emotion proactively to your task only and not to the people or situation. Focus on thinking to solve the problems. It is a mental exercise that increases mental strength and controls emotions.

2. Identifying your own emotion is not enough. Identifying other people's emotion on the same issue is equally important to reach a conclusive decision. This mental exercise increases your emotional intelligence to understand and manage both the people and the situation.

3. When you will be able to manage and control own emotion, you will achieve the ability to appreciate or cool off another people's emotion as well. This

exercise creates an emotional awareness in you and the emotional intelligence increases your level of performance.

- **Behavior** – The skills you develop in exercising the three above-mentioned mental exercises will help in all sphere of activities and relationships in your life. You will feel more considerate and compassionate which will help you to build a strong bonding in any kind of relationship. Your behavioral characteristic will rebuild.

  However, neither the people nor the situations allow you to keep going on. When one barrier after another come or all doors start closing, being a mentally strong person, you should not continue the task which may cost you more. It will be wise to quit the situation humbly and compromise the wrong path as it might lead to failure.

- **Confidence** – Confidence is believing in own mental strength and ability but not in an aggressive attitude. While you are exercising emotional intelligence and rebuilding behavioral characteristics successfully, you will be able to handle any social events, work, relationships, and family empathetically. Researchers have shown a person's brain thinks about 50,000 to 70,000 issues a day in which you boost yourself on thousands of issues while avoiding the rests with a fear of failure. So, exercising mental strength helps your brain to think the issues differently to be more productive instead of leaving the issues due to fear of failure and sporting an armor of confidence.

Importance of Mental Toughness

Every person has mental strength but it varies on the level of toughness that a person possesses. Higher the level you possess bigger the goals you achieve. Here, you will find the importance of mental toughness to be more productive and successful in life.

1. **Mental Strength Promotes Your Armor of Confidence** – When you ambitiously run behind a long-term goal, you may likely experience self-doubt at any point in time. Then. you should ask yourself about the ifs and buts that has brought a negative wave in you and created a low level of confidence. If you are mentally sound and strong, analyze the negative thoughts, adjust your attitude towards people and situation, and start working to march forward towards the goal. This will promote your mental strength with the armor of confidence and recharge motivation.

2. **Mental Ability Drives the Motivation** – When you stick to the goal, motivation plays the key role as driving force in you to keep moving on. However, psychologists

have shown that the graph of the motivation of a person is not linear rather it is a wave-like curved line. So, it has ups and downs. When motivation is at its peak, your mental strength is high enough to handle the people and situation. When it is at the bottom, you need to re-exercise the mental ability by digging deep into yourself to rediscover yourself. This practice will tune your motivation further.

3. **Mental Toughness Tunes Unhealthy Criticism** – Exercising mental strength helps you out to tune unhelpful advice and unworthy criticism from the people surrounding you. The mental ability helps to stay strong with the truth with values and emotions regardless of the criticisms thrown on you unless you make a mistake.

4. **Mental Power Helps to Learn from Mistakes** – When people judge something wrong, decide something wrong, apply something wrong, a mistake happens. Suppressing the mistake creates another wrongful action. A mentally sound person accepts mistakes humbly, analyze the mistake, identifies the cause of the mistake, and repairs the damage. This way you can get the courage to learn from the mistake.

5. **Mental Strength Imparts Courage** – In a long-term journey towards a goal, you may not stay all the time in a comfort zone. At one point of time or another, you need to move beyond the boundary. Practicing mental strength

regularly helps you to come up with the courage to go beyond and extend the boundary within your tolerance limit. However, you should keep a backup in case of any setback to avoid discomfort. This can increase your courage to move forward resiliently.

6. **Mental Power Helps to Bounce Back in Case of Setback** – Mentally weak people give up in case of any setback or failure without giving any effort for the next time. On the contrary, mentally strong people think that failures are the pillars of success. People work their mental power, analyze the causes of failure, tune the emotions, reconstruct the thoughts and get back from the failure by performing better than before. People with high mental power have a high level of self-worth and high tolerance level to accept failure regardless of being ridiculed by others. Regular exercising of mental power gives you the emotional strength to treat failure as throwing a stone to future success.

7. **Mental Power Controls Emotion** – In the para "Mental Ability Drives Motivation" above it is already explained that motivation can be high and low. Similarly, emotion gets high and low during the journey of activities in life. Thus, success also gets high and low as it is synchronized with emotion and motivation. If you do not have the skill to control the emotions, the temptation of the situation will control you and gratification from your

life will be a far-fetched dream. This situation invites immeasurable risks. Exercising the mental power is the key way to control your emotion, boost motivation, and build the path of success. Building mental power also helps you to develop a strong resilience to overcome the failure and bounce back with full confidence. This is an inevitable necessity of life to face the challenges in any sphere of activities.

"Do not judge me by my success, judge me by how many times I fell down and got back up again." — Nelson Mandela

Chapter 2

How To Boost Your Resilience?

Resilience is an exercise of mental ability that quickly helps you to adopt any adversity, potential threat, heartbreaking tragedy, traumatic event, or intense stress. All these may arise from a family relationship problem, or a workplace pandemonium and financial commotion. Adopting the situation means you are mentally getting back from the difficult situation to the environment just before the current stressful situation. A historical event, for example, can elaborate it. Americans were shocked like a thunderbolt on September 11, 2001, due to massive terrorist's attack but they came up from the traumatic situation within a very short time and rebuilt their lives as before. This is resilience. It did not mean the Americans did not face adversity and suffer pain. Resilience teaches a lesson that you have to keep on walking on the road of sufferings and pain to reach the goal.

Embrace the Changes in Your Life

Nobody likes failure. When you say you are at the top of the success, you mean, you have begun your career from the ground level, crossed the hurdles efficiently, and reached the top. So, for every up there is a down. The situation can change at any point in time. Change is a cyclical process. What is at the top today may come at the bottom tomorrow. Things which were comfortable yesterday can get rattled at any moment. Then there is a necessity for rebuilding the mental ability to come out of the situation. Are you not coping with the adversity or changes? Let's discuss a few important practices to increase your degree of resilience to embrace the changes.

- **Evaluate Your Degree of Control** – Sometimes you might have observed the people surrounding you are not trying to understand the change what is necessary. They are sticking to their habitual actions or attitude. What can you do under that situation? You can assess yourself about what and how far control you can take on the elements of change under that situation. Take responsibility to that extent only to mold the change and establish your competency.

- **Control Yourself After a Loss** – Life is full of change and every change has its transition. For example, when you were brought up you enjoyed your childhood but lost it forever when you entered into adolescence. There was a transition from childhood to adolescence. You missed your childhood but at the same time, you embraced the youth and celebrated it. More example can be cited like a breakup with your boyfriend or girlfriend, loss of a job, death of near and dear ones. Do you have faced any situation like that? You have to face a transition between before and after any loss occurred at all time. What is importantly necessary during a transitional phase is not to push yourself away into the grief that you might have felt from the situation. Accept the loss or change. You may seek support from your family members and close friends to control your emotion and rebuild your confidence.

- **Pull Yourself from the Past to Present and Set the Priorities** – Are you immersed into the past loss and grief. Pull yourself into the present and look around. New challenges are waiting for you which can open new opportunities. Look inside yourself. Find the strengths already in you. Set your priorities from the present. You have enough experience with your shortcomings from the past. So, get up and plan your strategy to fight the new challenges. You will find yourself as resilient and get back quickly with more mental strength than before.

Make Positive Connections

Resilience or come back from the difficulties requires a good association. An association means a combination of two or more things or persons. The positive connection has an association of two components. One is positivity and another one is connectivity. When these two components work together on you at a difficult time, you feel more resilient. However, the time requires to bring you back from a major set-back depends on the nature and amount of shock you absorbed from the past event.

Some examples are placed here to make you understand why recovery from the disaster depends on the gravity of the shock. Suppose one has lost a job. One has lost a near one. One has been abused for a long time in childhood.

In the first case, a loss of job happens at the adult age. Recovery of such loss will take little time if your family members and friends stay with you. When they boost you to find for a new job you will get additional strength in you. While getting boosted with additional mental strength, your search for a new job may be resolved within a short time.

In the second case, a loss of near one is a little bit different from that of the first case. Mental setback from the death of a near one may come at any point of time of your life. For the interest of the illustration, the time here is divided into two phases. One is childhood and adolescence period of your life and another one is adult and matured period of your life.

- During the first phase of your life, if death occurs to one of your parents, that brings a major shock to you. It is gross damage to a child's life. The child may recover the setback if the survivor parent and other family members positively nurture the child so that the child can feel that everybody is there to take care of him or her. In respect of the recovery time, it depends on how quickly the survivor parent and other family members can fill the gap created in the mind of the child due to the demise of one parent. It takes considerable time.

- During the second phase of life, you are adult and quite matured. You can recover yourself from such setback with the help of your family members and friends much earlier that the time what is required in case of a child and adolescent candidate.

In the third case, where a child has been abused for a long-time during childhood, it has a long-term impact on his or her mental status. Here, in this case, only the family member's support and assistance may not be sufficient to recover the child from his or her mental distress. The child additionally may need assistance from a professional psychologist who can bring back the child from the tremendous mental distress that he or she suffered in the past. The process may require a longer time than that required in the first and second case.

Whatever time is required in different cases as described above, two things are common in all cases. Positive thoughts and connecting with positive people are the key factors that play a vital role to make you resilient.

Become Goal-Oriented

You will not find a single person who never faces any sort of stressors during the entire life. So, the stressors are part of life. The problem is that sometimes people sink under the stressors and do not find a way to overcome the difficulties. Let's discuss how you can get out yourself from a difficult situation.

Be SMART – To be smart you should follow the SMART way which can make you resilient. The SMART is the acronym of five words viz., specific, measurable, attainable, realistic, and timely. The first two words are very close to each other. Unless you measure your goal, it will not be specific. Check if the goals set are attainable realistically and then only you can reach the goal in time. Suppose you want to save a certain amount of money within a set time limit. While doing so you might have to meet some other contingencies which might come on the way and you would not consider at the beginning of the savings program. This might happen due to your unrealistic savings target which is not commensurate with your lifestyle. So, to develop a realistic goal and to look forward, you must focus on your requirements more realistically. This way a continual step by step effort can strengthen you more to handle any momentary loss and achieve the ultimate goal.

Break Your Cycle of Negative Thinking

Do you have ever thought what plays in your mind that immerses you into a negative thought? A study was undertaken in the UK in 2013 to find out the underlying factors responsible for such negative thoughts. The data sample was collected from 30,000 people. The study revealed that self-blaming and rumination of past negative events of life plunged them into negative thinking. The eye of the researchers opened from the study. After detail analysis, they have suggested that cultivation of a positive mindset is the best counterpart of negative thinking. In the beginning, it may bring a small change but consistent mental exercise can navigate you to a strong positive mindset and help you to be resilient. Now let's see how that can be achieved.

- **Reframe Your Thoughts** – If you follow your day-to-day working environment minutely, you will find that you are used to embracing the situations and change your mindset. Suppose you are driving a car and you are hardly able to move due to heavy traffic. You have little time to reach the destination. In such a situation you can navigate the map to find out a bypass route and reach the destination. So, to reach the goal there must be at least more than one road. Now reframing your thoughts mean to choose the route that can show you the path to reach the goal. Selecting the right path to reach the goal is the reframing of positive thoughts.

- **Scan Positivity and Stay Obliged** – Psychology researchers suggest, you should spend a few minutes every day and just focus on your positive strength and stay grateful. If you practice it regularly for three weeks you will find that your brain has developed a pattern which helps you to scan all goodness in your surrounding world.

- **Nudge Your Brain Against Stress** – Research also says that you feel sufferings much more than the element of stressors exerts on you. This happens due to your way of thinking about the barriers that impact severely your mental health and wellbeing. So, when you feel stress try to focus on the elements of stress. You will find at least one or two ways, whatever little effort that maybe, that can reduce your stress and not allow you to sink into the stress. This way you can nudge your brain to avoid stress and bounce back to a positive zone to build a more resilient mindset.

- **Exercise Feel-Good Mental Habit** – Try to look everything easy, think easy, and act easy. You will feel goodness and happiness within you. This is one of the mental tonics that can increase your positivity and build a resilient mindset.

Take Action

One of the best ways to solve your problem reasonably and justifiably is to take proper action against the root cause of your distress. Below are the ways the psychologists commonly advise to solve your problem.

- **Identify the Problem** – Investigate the problem. You will find several issues that appear to you creating a problem. List all the issues. Define each issue separately and find why that issue is a problem for you. While defining the issues, focus on the behavioral aspect of the issue and not on a person or yourself. Suppose you have entered into a contract with a person who will work for you. You paid him some money in advance without any receipt. Then that fellow defrauded you. Being frustrated, you are telling now that "I was stupid". You are blaming yourself. Here, the true problem is not you but your behavior. You rely on people easily and quickly, allow them to betray and disappoint you.

- **Define the Purpose of Your Life** – Shake yourself from the inside. Ask yourself the purpose you want to serve in your life. Plan the purpose you want to attain realistically. Do not ask for more which is beyond your attainability capacity. For example, setting a goal to be happy in life is a broad aspect. Try to be specific. Try to find out your happiness. What and how you can do for that to be happier.

- **Brainstorming** – Are you in a deep problem? Do not hurry to solve the problem when you are in crisis. Take sufficient time, brainstorm as much as you can, take help of friends and family. Remember, some people will be always there to prevent your problem-solving effort and make the situation more difficult to handle. So, try to sort out three to four varying alternative ways while resolving your difficulty.

- **Assess Each Alternative** – Assess each alternative that you have framed as discussed in the previous para. Measure each solution in terms of its positive effect and negative impact along with risk factor associated with it.

- **Choose the Solution** – After assessing all the alternatives you can find which solution can bring you maximum favorable condition. Remember not all favorable condition can give you the maximum satisfaction. So, find out which solution can project your happiness more with minimum negative consequences. Then set a timeline within which you can accomplish the ultimate goal.

- **Execute the Chosen Solution** – Actively move forward with your chosen solution and do not look back. You must lead towards the goal without worrying about any potential threat.

- **Evaluate the Action** – At the end of the execution of the chosen solution, evaluate your action. If you succeed, you will get back your confidence and feel to be resilient. If failed, do not worry, you must have mistaken to choose the right solution. You will learn many things from your mistake and start again from the beginning.

Always Be Optimistic

If you develop a habit to watch the brighter aspect of things regularly, you will feel more optimism in you than others who has no experience of such exercise. This habit enhances your positive mindset and provides health benefit also. Now, let's see how optimism provides some advantages over the negative thoughts.

- **Health Benefit** – A study was undergone on 99 students of Harvard University to test how optimism impacts the general health condition. The study revealed that the students who used to believe in optimism at their age of 25 years were found significantly healthier at their age between 45 and 60 that the students who were pessimists. Another study revealed people lead a pessimistic lifestyle highly suffer from poor health, infectious diseases, and earlier mortality.

- **Optimism Helps to Achieve Greater** – In a sport like a football or cricket, teamwork is necessary. It is found optimistic sportsperson can create greater positive synergy in the team and achieve better performance than a pessimistic sportsperson. Additionally, pessimistic sportsperson, who use to think from the beginning that he or she may perform worse, is more prone to the poorest performance.

- **Persistence** – An optimist never quits even under pressure whereas, a pessimist often surrenders and quits. A good example is that the US President Donald Trump despite has been bankrupted many times never quit his business. He has been able to fight the odds with persistence and turn his failure into millions and millions of dollars. This is an example of mental resilience too.

- **Strengthens Mindset** – In a medical study, depressed patients were treated a cognitive therapy to reframe their thought process (which is already discussed under "Break Your Cycle of Negative Thinking"). It was found that reframing thought training to the depressed persons worked more viably than the drug. Such training strengthens the mindset of depressed patients. Optimism lasts for a long time and helps to fight against any future setback.

- **Lessens Stress** – Research shows that people having optimism are much proactive to any work and thus they experience less stress than the pessimists. This happens because optimists rely on their abilities and persistence. They have a win-win attitude and self-reliance to handle any minor setback. As they belong to a robust mindset, they can take the risk to create positive results in their lives.

Indulge in Proper Self-Care

To keep your well-being balanced, true care of yourself is an integral part of your life. People usually involve themselves with different activities to get refreshed like a massaging, dine out, two-three days travelling etc. However, when self-care is concerned, more elements can be included in it which essentially helps to increase your resilience. Let's discuss those powerful elements for boosting your confidence.

- **Stop Comparison** – Everywhere in the workplace, social gatherings, social media people use to measure happiness and success based on another people's life. They only discuss success without knowing the whole scenario of the success story of the people who made success possible. Comparison creates temptation, anxiety, and insecurity in you. So, stop comparing yourself with others. Instead, you put your inner strength to unlock your thoughts and apply it so that you can potentially achieve your mission.

- **Replacing Self-Criticism Develop New Attitude** – Sometimes people become tougher on themselves which results in reinforcement of negative aspects on their mindset. Self-criticism sometimes may be tricky and drain out your positive thought. Do you have experienced this before? Self-care coaching can replace your self-criticism and catch your inner positive strength. So, develop an attitude that can act as a stopper to your self-criticism.

- **Be Quiet and Listen to Your Heart** – While staying alone for some hours, you might have felt that your emotional intelligence supplies many effective choices to perform more better on day-to-day work. Later on, you apply those choices on daily routine work and get success. This indicates that if you take some time on any issue and think about it quietly, you can connect and interact with the people properly. Deep listening habit is another self-care technique that can reduce the scope of misunderstanding and stress arises from it.

- **Forgiveness** – It is quite natural that few vulnerable issues will take a longer time than any other issues. So, you need to be patient. It is worth remembering that forgiveness releases your pain and helps you to regain your mental peace. If you allow yourself focusing on thinking what worse has happened, you will not be able to look forward and lose your resilience. So, to know your mental ability and increase your emotional intelligence under a vulnerable situation, forgiveness acts a medicine for maintaining your deeper peace and feel better.

Know Yourself

Being brought up and grown-up by your parents from a kid to an adult does not mean that you know yourself. It is a process of understanding own self. It needs a conscious effort. Without knowing yourself, sooner or later, you will fall in frustration of life. Here you can get to know how to know yourself.

- **Understand Your Personality** – Understanding the characteristics of your own is the first key to know your personality. You might have collected other peoples' views which is a different issue because all those are their opinion.

  The question is who you are as a person. Understanding the way of reaction to innumerable situations that you face in everyday life by asking yourself "Why and how have I done that?" and answering to it is a great exercise.

  It is also important to know how you feel yourself amongst your friends and what you feel amongst strangers. Precisely, what you portray about your persona to the people. What you exactly like to do on a rewarding day and as well as on failure day which indicates how you react to your surrounding world.

- **Understand Your Core Values** – In simple word, core value relates to what is right and what is wrong. When you say something morally right that comes from the core of your heart. That is the core value. Core values are ethics and culture of your own that creates ideological integrity in you. When you decide something good or bad, you do so by filtering your beliefs and values you already possess. Suppose, a thief has stolen some valuables. In this incident, you are telling that stealing is wrong. Fine, but think deeply that stealing is not exactly a value. The value here would be what the thief has tried to achieve by committing the act stealing. So, the value you possess in the core of your heart helps you to survive in agreement with others.

- **Understand Your Physique** – The physique you belong is yours. Your mind and soul are within your body. The more you learn about your body the more you reach to your soul. When you reach out to your soul you will know yourself more in every breath, you can understand your ability as well as disability, your flexibility as well as rigidity. A strong body gives birth to a strong mind and a strong mind possesses a sound soul. A sound soul searches for pure knowledge and replaces your enemy the illusion. When you can come out of the illusion of the situation, your mind shows you the right path and tells you about what to do and how to do. Your body gets ready to act or perform.

- **Understand Your Dreams** – As soon as you get to know your own body, mind, and soul you can identify your dream of a life that matters you most. Now it is time to know the details of your dream. Specify your requirements to fulfil your dream, your likes and dislikes towards the journey of your life. Suppose your dream is to be a musician. Then, ask yourself about which musical instrument you like most and how far proficiency you want achieve. Make your dream to be successful by pursuing it as a daily routine.

Develop a Sense of Humor

In today's life, you cannot avoid stress in any way but can manage it by adopting some techniques. Applying a sense of humor can act as an amazing defense line when you are not getting through the stress. Developing a sense of humor at the face of stress while dealing with life's challenges is a great thing. It helps you to improve your physical and as well as mental health. It also helps you to:

- Make bonding with other people
- Look things in a separate way
- Gather experience normally
- Keep a strong relationship with others

However, developing a good sense of humor is not difficult but it needs a little but a persistent practice. Few such ways are discussed here to cope with stresses.

- **Begin with a Smile** – Start work with a smiling face. The smile on your face has the power to melt down the stress involved in the work. After completion of the work with a smiling face, even if the work is too stressful, you will feel happiness. If you cannot smile at the beginning then at least pretend to smile. Pretention of smiling will create a habit in you to work with a smiling face and you will feel greater comfort in the face of stressful work.

- **Step Back Under Too Hard Situation** – If you fall within too much difficulty which may appear to be overwhelming you should immediately step back from the situation. Sometimes, solving a problem by cracking a situation becomes more stressful when you try repeatedly on the same issue. Take a short break for two or three days. View the entire situation. Place yourself in a neutral position without any bias. Now observe every stage of the event with a fresh eye. You will find a new frame in which you can get the exact solution.

- **Associate with Funny friends** – An association with friends having a strong sense of humor can help you to reduce your stress. They can refresh you when you are feeling a heavily heavy heart under tremendous pressure and anxiety.

- **Read Humor Story** – Reading a humor story can also help you to come out of the unbearable stress. Humor story presents serious things with a light-hearted view. If you can develop a reading habit of humor books, you will find yourself strength to see a serious thing in a different way which may not appear as stressful as you have seen it before.

"The secret of life, though, is to fall seven times and to get up eight times." — Paulo Coelho

Chapter 3

Train Your Brain For Mental Toughness

Train your brain is necessary to stay calm under pressure. It helps you to increase your mental toughness. In case of any disaster, it helps you to look beyond what happened. It gives you prudence to observe the elements of disaster with a new lens, review your thoughts, get the shortcomings, recompose the actionable parts in a new frame and get the work done seamlessly. However, life does not always follow an easy-going road and everyone has to face failure. So, do not worry about your failure or do not feel sad due to failure. Your mental strength is actually your true friend who always stays with you like your shadow. It stays with you in success and as well as failure. So, it is always with and all you need to strengthen it more.

Know the Difference Between Ruminating and Problem-Solving

Like any other person, you also recall the past event of your life and reflect your previous behavior in a present event which is similar to the past one. This is common to all. You must remember that while understanding your previous experience in one incident helps you to make more informed decisions on a similar occasion in the future.

However, on many occasions in which it is seen wandering in the past creates a situation more complex than the past situation and people shatter in the present occasion. This happens because people like to travel in the past and try to find out the answers to too many questions from the failure of the previous occasion. Ultimately, they fall into the trap of chewing the cud of past events. They even do not try to explore the abilities they have to solve the problem in the present situation. Additionally, they reflect their experience and relate the same in the present occasion. This way they force themselves to run into the harsh and unpleasant cycle of rumination. This creates an immense negative impact on their mindset and prolongs for a considerable time. As a result, they immerse themselves in a deep depression and even get detached from their close family members and friends.

Now, how can you get to know if you are engaging yourself in an adaptive self-analysis of the past event to solve the present problem or in a maladaptive rumination? Possibly the answer is within you. So, the best way is to ask yourself if your thought process is helping you to solve the present problem or in fact, it is challenging your potential ability to handle the present situation. Asking yourself this question is very important to you because when you ruminate an issue, you only focus on your critical thoughts. This is the thought process that prevents you to come up with the right solution in the present situation. Although you might have tried to solve the problem still you become unable to find out an effective solution because of your mindset that has been trapped into a vicious cycle.

Different studies have made to understand the link between a rumination condition and the difficulties to solve the problems. The studies revealed that the persons who fell under a rumination condition were less able to handle their present problems. On the contrary, those who could divert the experience of failure to adopt in the present situation were more able to solve their present problems. So, it is always suggested when you fall under rumination, immediately take a break from the situation. Divert your concentration on other things. Read a humor book or participate in entertainment with families or friends. Refresh your mindset. Then analyze your present problem. Find out your abilities to solve the problem.

Practice Meditation

It has been proved time and again that meditation can improve the level of mental toughness you have. Even soldiers who are about to go on a mission or are being trained for combat are advised to practice meditation and for good reason. They do not become too emotional in their career or in other words, their mental toughness is improved.

In the world of mental toughness, there are usually three types of people. The first one is the marshmallow. As the name suggests, these people are very soft, both inside out and so any little amount of pressure on them can cause havoc. The next group of people is the jelly beans. They have a soft inner core but a hard shell. They are obviously tougher than marshmallows but at times, even they can buckle up after a prolonged period of stress. The last group of people is the rocks, who can literally handle everything that is put in front of them. They are not only hard from the outside but also from the inside.

When a person learns to adopt a lifestyle that includes a regular time set aside for meditation, then he/she eventually starts developing a growth mindset. In this mindset, people do not see their failures or obstacles as negative things but rather learn from their mistakes and events of life. You will learn to harness the power of meditation and then use that energy to stay positive throughout your day. Your idea of mental toughness will be elevated to a whole new level with this new routine of meditation.

At an average, a person has over 70,000 thoughts in a day. What meditation does is that it helps you seek that quiet place inside your head that is present but is hidden under the pressure of all those thoughts weighing you down. But people often confuse meditation with mindfulness. Mindfulness is a different thing and you can say that it is a type of meditation. But with the help of meditation, you will be able to analyze so many thoughts that got buried in your subconscious and you will be able to do so without being judgmental at all.

The first way in which meditation promotes mental toughness is that it helps you enter a state of calmness. When you are calm, you have the time and concentration required to judge which thoughts are worthy of your attention and thus you can invest your time in them. You will also learn a rational way to respond to anxiety in your daily life. Moreover, with meditation, you can distinguish between noise and static. Your recalling power will increase and you will also learn how you can control your mind so that you do not get affected by any distractions. In short, meditation can improve your capacity to handle stress and thus enhance your level of mental toughness.

Don't Beat Yourself Up For Things You Cannot Control

There will always be things in your life that are beyond your control and this is the ultimate truth. If you cannot make peace with this fact, then you will have a tough time on this planet.

When people cannot get over the fact that they can't control everything, they end up becoming control freaks.

Thus, if you want to train your brain to have mental toughness, then you need to stop picking fights on every small matter that comes your way. Frankly, you need to understand that everything is not worth it to waste your energy fighting over it. There will always be some troubling times that you have to face in your life. But don't fret or don't give in to depression just because you cannot control the situation. The simple fact is that the situation cannot be controlled. And when something goes wrong, don't beat yourself up for something that didn't happen because of you.

Yes, you can influence people but you can never or rather you should never force your will upon others. For example, you can do everything you can to make the party good but you cannot do anything to make the people have fun. It is their own decision and choice. Sometimes, the feeling of being a control freak intensifies even more when you have the tendency to jump to catastrophic outcomes which might not even happen. So, judge your thoughts and think whether you are indulging in such a practice or not. If you are, then think about what is the worst that can practically happen. Usually, it won't be as bad as you are thinking it to be.

You also need to have a stress management plan. As already mentioned in the previous point, you can practice meditation or you can also do something you love. Practice anything that is stress-relieving to you. You can even go out and have a good time with your friends if that is what you want. Create your own positive affirmations that you can tell yourself in a situation of stress. For example, if you are thinking 'Important members of the board are going to be present at the meeting' then you need to tell yourself 'I can handle it'.

Engage in Third-Person Self-Talk

Do you often remember all the saddening or painful experiences of your past? Then, self-talk from a third-person perspective can be really helpful in such situations. Moreover, psychologists have stated it as a crucial method of self-regulation. Everyone has anxiety-inducing contexts but third-person self-talk can help you combat them. When you are speaking to yourself in third-person, you are actually distancing yourself from your own mind and this can help you judge yourself less emotionally. Every emotion has its own perceived intensity but all that can be lessened if you try seeing it from a third-person perspective.

If you want to solidify your long-term emotional, cognitive and behavioral goals, then indulging in positive self-talk can help you achieve that. Now if you are wondering how third-person self-talk is done, then you must know that it is quite simple. The usage of first-person pronouns like I, my or me is restricted. Rather, you should be using pronouns like 'she', 'he', 'it' or your name. In some way, a third-person self-talk session can promote you to think in a way that you do about others. In short, you will be viewing yourself just like you view others. And so, this will, in turn, promote self-control by giving you the much needed emotional distance.

You can practice this form of emotional regulation if you are someone who is coping with some intense feeling or is trying to control your emotions or anxiety or even depression for that matter. Thus, third-person self-talk can come in quite handy and it is something that you should add to your mental tools arsenal because it can not only increase your level of mental toughness but also help you cope with a lot of problems that can come your way.

Give a Name To Your Emotions

Dealing with your emotions is important in all aspects of your life and not only when it comes to mental toughness. When you name your emotions, the process is called labeling and it is also the first step for everyone towards effectively dealing with their emotions. It might sound easy to you now but it is way tougher in reality. You have to pinpoint what it is that you are feeling and sometimes you might label your emotions as something that it is not.

There are so many reasons as to why labeling your emotions is a difficult task. For starters, right from your childhood, you have been taught that it is necessary to suppress your strong emotions. Moreover, sometimes there are unspoken organizational and societal rules that stop you from expressing your actual feelings. Or sometimes a child is never actually taught in what way they should speak up and express what they are feeling. All of these things cumulatively act as a barrier to correct labeling of emotions.

The most common emotions that are visible in a workplace setting are stress and anger or at least that is what they are labeled as. But in most cases, these two labels mask way deeper emotions than they actually seem to be. The tendency to avert from showing or talking about one's emotions is a growing concern in today's world especially when mental health issues are increasing each day. When you avoid speaking about your emotions, you automatically create a distance between you and your emotions. This affects your ability to identify how you are feeling at a particular moment.

As already mentioned above, sometimes adults do end up labeling their emotions but they do it in the wrong way. For example, if someone is feeling sad, then instead of saying 'I'm feeling low' they might say 'My eyes got watery, nothing more'.

Do you see the difference between the two ways of expression? You must spend some time every day with yourself and you must acknowledge the fact that you are feeling what you are feeling. You should also think about how these emotions affect or are going to affect your decision-making abilities. Whether it is about something that happened in your workplace or your personal life, if you have some emotion on your mind, it is more likely to get spilled all over your life and create havoc.

When it comes to your emotions, you need to concentrate on developing a more nuanced vocabulary. I am not saying this just because I want you to be precise. No, that is not what I mean. What I mean is that when you use the right vocabulary, you will also gain the power of describing your emotions correctly. Correct diagnosis of your emotions is essential if you want to respond correctly to them. Also, don't stick to basic descriptions like angry or sad as sometimes your emotions are way more intense than that. There is a variety of flavors and levels of every emotion. Being angry might also mean that you are grumpy or annoyed. You need to label your emotions the way they are.

Maintain a Balance in Your Emotions With the Help of Logic

Whether it is a family dilemma or a financial crisis where you need to make important decisions, being mentally strong is very important. But for that, you need to implement logic to balance your emotions. So, if you see that your emotions are running high, take a stand immediately and increase your level of rational thinking. If you are confused as to how you can achieve this in your life then here is a tip that works for most people – whenever you are making a choice, consider the pros and cons and write them down somewhere. When you finish your list of pros and cons and read it again, you will realize many things and may even be able to separate your emotions from your decisions.

Decisions are something you cannot spend your day without. Even if you are not doing anything and simply chilling at home, there will be several decisions cropping up in your mind, for example, 'what should I eat for lunch?' Do you see? Your daily life is filled with so many such small and big decisions that sometimes we even tend to look past them. If you are planning to quantify your decisions in a day, then don't try to walk on that path because it is nearly impossible. Your decisions are not always huge. They can even be hidden in mundane things like whether you want to get a coffee or make yourself some tea.

It is often said that 80% of the choices made by humans are influenced by their emotions. So, do you favor logic or emotion when you are making some decisions in your life? Unsavory situations in life can arise at any moment and they are all due to momentary lapses in your judgment. Yes, you might feel constant friction in your mind when you are trying to create a balance between emotions and logic and your emotional self might even try to break free and dominate, but you have to deal with it all if you want to achieve mental toughness.

Practice Gratitude

There are so many benefits to expressing and practicing gratitude on a daily basis and it also has proven its usefulness when it comes to mental toughness. According to a study, people who practice gratitude are found to be 25% happier than others who don't. People usually have a tendency to focus more on their obstacles and less on all the good things in life. But you have to practice gratitude and feel happy for all that you have because there are so many people out there who crave what you have. This transition is not going to be easy but nothing is impossible if you try hard.

You need to figure out ways in which you can widen your scope of self-assessment. So, the first step is to identify all those things in your life for which you are grateful. When you acknowledge the fact that you are grateful for certain things in your life, then you will also start taking steps to improve your standing within those circumstances. Moreover, the more effort you put, the more positive outcomes you will get and you will have much more to be grateful for. You can also maintain a gratitude diary where you will write down all your thoughts and things that you are grateful for. You can even go through this diary when you are low and you will instantly have a smile on your face.

You can also make it your mantra to thank at least one person the moment you step out of your house. The way you speak can also go a long way in helping you to practice gratitude. If you reach somewhere late and someone is waiting for you, then you can say 'Thank you for waiting for me' instead of 'I'm sorry I kept you waiting'. All these small gestures definitely matter in the bigger picture. You can also call up someone and tell them thank you for something they have done for you or simply for being with you.

Volunteering is also one of the things that can help you feel grateful. If there is a cause that you believe, find events that are taking place in your town or city and volunteer in those events. The happiness and satisfaction that you will feel later is totally something else and will also increase your resilience. Practice complimenting others freely. This will make you feel good. There can be so many ways in which you can practice these random acts of kindness and you should do so in whichever way you can.

Go Out of Your Comfort Zone

Everyone has his/her comfort zones and they are called so because a person feels comfortable and safe in those moments.

But along with that sense of safety also comes stagnation which can shun your growth. You will not be able to make the best use of the opportunities that come your way if you decide not to leave your comfort zone. You shouldn't cow away from things just because they are unfamiliar to you.

Whether it is starting a project that you had been thinking about for quite a long time or whether it is about reaching out to new contacts, you should do what you want. But in order to change your mentality, it might take you some time but trust me, it will be worth it when you do. The first thing that you should start is studying all your physical manifestations of the fear that you feel inside. When you understand what are the signs of discomfort that you feel then you will be able to identify when you are out of your comfort zone. Replace all the disempowering thoughts that you are having with positive and empowering ones. Say you to yourself 'I am fearless' and make it your mantra.

If you learn to seek new experiences and challenges then you will become way more resilient and mentally tougher than those who remain stuck in one point in life. You can either choose to stretch your abilities to achieve a growth mindset or you can choose to become stagnated for the rest of your life. You will be automatically achieving way higher levels in your personal and professional life when you learn to break your own mold. Embrace all the discomfort that comes your way. Remember that if there is any catalyst for growth, discomfort is one of them. It will force you to adapt and learn new things to increase your potential.

There are so many things that we keep avoiding in our daily lives but the secret to success often lies in those same things. If long-term success is what you have been dreaming about, then you need to stop avoiding things and go out of your comfort zone. It is in the human nature that when you are challenged, you will automatically turn towards acquiring new skills and looking for newer perspectives. This will help you push your boundaries. On the other hand, when you keep repeating the same tasks, your comfort boundaries get enhanced and if you think of this the other way then – if you keep practicing your discomforts enough, soon they will be included within your comfort boundaries.

Reframe Your Negative Thoughts

This is something similar to not thinking about things that you cannot control. In this exercise, you are going to identify all the negative thoughts that you are having and then replace them with positive ones. Everyone falls prey to negative thinking. It is something that is very difficult to avoid for most people. So, what you need to do is start developing productive thinking that can replace your negative thinking habits.

It doesn't matter what is going on in your life. There is always a way to reframe the current situation. So, it is always in your hand and it will always be your choice to the way you want to think about what is currently happening. You can choose to make yourself feel better instead of drowning in your own anxiety, sorrow or whatever it is that you are feeling. In simpler terms, whenever you are reframing a current situation, you are simply changing your perspective of viewing that situation and nothing else. But this small change can do wonders. This will prevent you from getting caught up in any of the day-to-day problems in your life. Sometimes, stressful situations can block you from doing better in life and a way to avoid that from happening is to come up with a better perspective.

If you are clueless about how you can achieve this, then don't worry, the process is quite simple. Notice when you are having a negative thought and then ask yourself in what way can you reframe the thought that you are having. You can also think about the worst that could have happened but didn't. Say to yourself – 'at least X thing did not happen.' You can flip the situation at hand and make it positive in your mind.

Another way of bringing out the positivity from every situation is to think about how it has helped you or what you have learned from the event. Every situation in life, no matter how bad it is, will always give you a lesson and if you can take it then you will no longer see that particular situation in a negative light. You need to remember that sometimes the most important pre-requisite for success is failure and this same failure will help you move forward in your endeavor.

So, whenever you are having some unhelpful thoughts in your mind, it is time that you take a stand and develop some rational and realistic thoughts. Your brain is not always right so even if it tells you that you are not going to get a job, keep applying for various positions and you will. No good will come to you if you keep investing all your energy into your negative thoughts. So, instead of wasting your energy, use it to at least try and give your best in what you are doing.

"Mental toughness is a state of mind - you could call it character in action." – Vince Lombardi

Chapter 4

Discover How To Be Relentless With True Mindset

Before we start with the ways in which you can become relentless, you need to understand what it truly means to be relentless. The word 'relentless' is very commonly used in the world of sports and it is used to refer to those who are very much competitive and intense. But the word is applicable in real life as well and it is used to refer to those who are determined about achieving the end result no matter what. It is more like a state of mind that will help you achieve all that you want and be successful and not stop at any of the barriers that come your way. It will also help you to stay strong when others around you are falling weak to the circumstances.

So, if you are wondering how to become relentless even in the face of adversity then here is how you can do it.

Learn to Take Responsibility

Whether you are running a business or working in an office, you need to learn to be responsible for your own actions. You need to take charge. You have to decide how you want to get the job done and then you need to be determined about figuring out ways in which you can achieve it. Learning to take personal responsibility is what helps you succeed in life. It is quite obvious and yet deceptive that success will always start and end with you.

When you have something on your mind and you want to be successful at it, it is you who are responsible for both your success and failure. Yes, you will face barriers and yes, there will be people by your side who will be there to help you out. But that is it. No matter how many doors they open for you, it is you alone who will have to walk through that door to reach your goal. The first step always has to be taken by you. You might even have to make some hard choices along the way but you need to take 100% responsibility for everything that leads you to your dream. Here are some of the things that you can do to start taking responsibility –

- **Make the decision** – Making the decision will always be the first step that you have to take. It will feel a daunting step and it is completely normal to feel so. When you are about to tell yourself about the things that you want to achieve and the person you want to be, it is a huge shift. You need to look at yourself in the mirror and say to yourself that gone are the days when excuses were all that you had. You need to stop blaming others for what is happening in your life. Just go ahead and make the decision that from today, you are the only one who will be responsible for your success.

- **Set the boundaries** – But when you are making decisions, you also need to learn to set a few boundaries. Visualize your success in your mind in your free time and then think about all those things that are causing you to be frustrated or distracted. When you figure that out, it is time for you to eliminate some of those distractions from your life. Once this is done, it is time for you to analyze your personal relationships. You will see that some people are hindering your success and you need to maintain some soft boundaries with them.

- **Turn to an active approach** – Are you someone who spends long hours pondering over what to do rather than doing the task itself? Then you need to start developing an active approach in life. Talking about your goals and successes definitely feels good but do you know what feels even better? Taking action towards achieving those goals. Do you know why? This is because whenever you are taking some action, you are also about to get a result.

- **It is okay to change your direction** – You need to understand the difference between what you should do and what you want to do. What you should do is what others or society wants you to do but what you want to do is your passion and it is something that will keep you going. If you ever find yourself comparing to others, you need to nip that practice in the bud. When you are personally responsible for your actions, you also need to understand that it is completely okay to change your direction.

- **Never forego your integrity** – When you learn to live with integrity, that is when you are truly taking responsibility for everything that is happening in your life. What are the promised that you have made in your life? Have you kept all of them? One of the cornerstones of success is nothing but integrity. So, drop the blame game and ditch all those petty excuses if you truly want to be responsible.

Drop Your Excuses

One of the reasons why people are not relentless and they give up on their goals too easily is because they are so fond of their excuses that they simply cannot leave them behind. If you want to build self-discipline, there is no short cut to it. You need to learn how you can drop your excuses and only then can you make the most out of your life.

So, if you want to drop your excuses, you need to start by identifying them. Think about all the excuses that you have been giving yourself lately. It might be something that you are delaying for a long time or it can also be something that you are telling yourself as a reason for your unhappiness. Whatever it is, you need to write them down in a piece of paper. Now that you are aware of your excuses, take a moment and see what you are feeling. Are you feeling uneasy? Well, there is nothing unusual in it. Remember how we already spoke in the previous chapter that you need to go out of your comfort zone if you want to excel? That is all you have to do here.

Now, you need to cross all those excuses out of your list. You need to take a mental stand that after today, you are not going to make those excuses ever again and saying this is not enough. You have to follow this decision through and stick to it with integrity. Another thing that you can do is for every excuse on your list, take positive action. In this way, you will find yourself one step ahead of where you were yesterday. Now all of this will not be easy and you also need to prepare yourself so that you are ready to take every challenge that you face. You need to remember that excuses are only distractions and if you stick to them, you will not achieve any progress in life at all.

Do you want to reach your goals and go ahead from where you already are? Then you need to start focusing on all those tasks you have at hand and stop worrying about the trillion excuses that are cropping up in your mind. Everyone would have been so rich in the world if excused could have been counted as currency. But since they are not, if you think closely, excuses don't really offer any help or value when it comes to your success. They only hinder your pace. You also need to surround yourself with people who believe in you and who will motivate you to work harder. If your life is full of open loops, you will never be able to reach your ultimate goal.

Stop sugar-coating every mistake you make in life. Instead, start analyzing your mistakes and learn from them. Acknowledge that you have made a mistake because it is completely normal. No one is flawless. When you say that your plan has not gone the way it was supposed to be then there is nothing to be ashamed of. People will respect you for taking responsibility for your actions.

Stop Looking for Shortcuts

You will often find others asking those who have already succeeded that what is the secret to their success. Well, according to me, there is never a secret or shortcut to success. It is quite simple. You work hard, you succeed. There is no other way to this. There are no magic tricks that will transport you to your dream reality. If you have a goal, visualize it and think about all those steps that are necessary to be taken. Then you need to ask yourself honestly, whether you really want to do all that it takes to reach the goal. There are no hacks to completing your journey faster than others. The journey has importance because it teaches you a lot of lessons you will need later on and so you need to experience the journey and stop looking for shortcuts.

The culture of today's world is obsessed with all types of shortcuts in life but they will never get you anywhere in your future. There is an immense amount of increase in the rebuttal of experiential value, intolerance for hard work, an instant want for gratification, and a shrinking span of attention among everyone. Everyone shows this imperative need for immediacy in all spheres of their life. You will see so many people wanting those six-pack abs overnight but not with consistent effort. You cannot finger snap your way to everything.

Yes, all of this is nothing new. This was present in older days as well. Only the mode of presentation has changed and the intensity has increased as well. But if you crave for a relentless attitude, then you need to stop looking for shortcuts. You need to work your way through all the struggles in your life and achieve that goal you have been dreaming of. The concept of hacks and shortcuts completely overlooks how important the journey is and the paramount role it plays in shaping the character of a person preparing him/her for their role. If you are truly passionate about something, then you should be seeking the experience and not willing to jump at the shortcut the first chance you get.

You need to have goals because they will keep you going. Your goals and dreams are the drivers on your path because of which you will never stop. But at the same time, you also need to distance yourself from the idea of the end result. The expectation for what you are going to get in the end is what makes you want to rush everything. Don't get me wrong. You need to have goals but what I am asking you to do is stop thinking about end results because they are as irrelevant as a third-party comment. You will learn a lot of things during your journey and in the end, you will be a completely different person and you never know how you will be viewing the world then.

You might even need to work extra hours but when you love something, all of this should not mean hard work. You should be more than willing to walk that extra mile if it means that you will be closer to success. You might be falling multiple times but you have to pick yourself up and keep walking on the path. Nobody will be looking at you while you are doing all this hard work and you should still be doing it – for yourself. You have to make progress no matter how slow it is but it has to be incremental.

Do Your Work

As we have already talked about the fact that there is no shortcut to success, then what is it that you should actually do? The answer is right there in front of your eyes. Work! But this does not necessarily mean that you have to burn yourself out and work day and night in order to achieve what you want. You simply have to work smart and love what you are doing. Yes, this might also involve you working way more than others but only to the point you can. You should not get yourself overworked and affect your physical or mental health.

Dreams are obviously great but don't get stuck in daydreaming while your thoughts remain inside your head. You need to turn your thoughts into actions. Wishing that you will achieve your dream one day will never make you reach that level of success magically. You have to work for it. Working with all your effort will improve your chances of achieving all that you want in life. But if you are giving all that effort without any positive strategy, then too you are not getting any results out of it. You need to have a solid strategy and you also need to work on it.

Also, you have to be consistent with what you are doing. You cannot do something today and leave it tomorrow and then wait for results to be in your favor. No matter which successful person you ask, all of them will give you the same answer that they have worked day and night for achieving what they have today and it was not built in a day. They had to give the same amount of effort to their work on a daily basis. If you want to be relentless, then you cannot afford to back down or accept anything less than what you deserve. Firstly, you need to be one hundred percent sure about what you want and secondly, you need to fully believe in your abilities and that you can do it.

People are usually pretending to be relentless whereas, in reality, all they want is their work for the day to be over so that they can go out and party. But passionate and successful are those who believe in the power of that one BIG dream which they are pursuing with all their hearts and mind. You cannot convince anyone that you are a relentless person when it comes to your job when you only spend a couple of hours in a day for it. Sometimes, you might find yourself stuck in a single strategy that is not even working out well for you. If you find yourself in such a situation then it is time for you to gear up and make some changes. It is time for you to change your strategy.

Push Yourself

There will always be something in your day that you have to do but you don't actually want to do it. And mind it; it is going to happen every day. But you need to push yourself and challenge yourself to be uncomfortable and be okay with it. You need to break the barrier of apathy and fear and laziness that is holding you back. So, in short being uncomfortable will be a part of your daily routine and you have to push your feelings aside and still keep walking. That is what being relentless means.

There will be times when you will think that you can't do something but every time, you will have to push harder and make it happen. Whether it is that last minute or that last task, you should complete everything that you thought you would in a day. Whether it is the first hour of the day or the last, you have to maintain the same intensity in your efforts. Limits are created by your own mind and if you truly believe in your abilities then you can easily move past all your limits. When you do this consistently, you will notice how your new normal will be actually your old limits.

That is how you develop a growth pattern. You need to push your boundaries and make them bigger. Think of it this way – if you are practicing the same set of exercises every day, would that do you any good? No, because in the long term, you will stagnate and that is exactly what happens to you in real life too. If you feel that you cannot meet the deadline today, then you need to try and push your limits. People usually have the zeal to work harder in their earlier stages of life when they have just set foot on the road towards success but as the days go by, they start forgetting the fire in their eyes and seek comfort.

One of the key rules of pushing yourself is to first have something in which you strongly believe. If your purpose is not strong enough, you will never develop the work-hard mentality and you will always feel like taking breaks. Having small goals is not what a strong purpose means. A strong purpose is something that is going to impact your life in a huge way and will bring a largely positive change. You should also try and read and watch stuff that is inspirational and will keep you motivated. They will eliminate all the discouragement that you have accumulated. You also need to visualize yourself working hard and achieving your dreams.

Another important thing is to eliminate all lazy people from your people or at least try and stay away from them. When you mix with people who are lazy, you will no doubt develop a tendency to become lazy yourself or start procrastinating. But when you have people who are hard-working, they will inspire you to work hard too. So, having these go-getters in your life can also push you towards your goal. Moreover, if they sense that you are becoming lazy, they might end up abandoning you and that too will keep you working towards your dream.

"You must be passionate, you must dedicate yourself, and you must be relentless in the pursuit of your goals. If you do, you will be successful." – Steve Garvey

Chapter 5

Do These 13 Things to Become Unbeatable With An Unstoppable Mind

You will come across so many people in your life who have this unbeatable attitude and when they are determined that they are going to get something, they simply go and get it. To them, every day is equally important because they are always doing something productive as they have an unstoppable mind. They are also mentally strong otherwise maintaining this attitude wouldn't have been possible. So, if you want to become like this as well, here are 13 things that you should do.

Develop the Freedom to Act on Instinct

The first step towards becoming truly unstoppable is to develop an attitude where you have complete trust in yourself. You need to be the master of the craft that you are pursuing and why shouldn't you be? You are doing it all day and you are spending hours perfecting it. This act should come to a point where you don't have to think. You will simply know what you are doing and you can act based on that. That is what is known as trusting your instincts – that feeling within which tells you what to do.

You will often find people telling you that they are successful today because they listened to their inner voice. You have to do exactly that. Listen to what your gut is telling you to do. You fail only when you think that you have already lost. Until then, you are still on the battlefield. Everything is in your mindset. If you think that this is the end of the world, it sure will be but if you think that you can make it till the end, you will. If you are facing difficulty in following your instincts, then you need to commit yourself fully. When you do that, you'll know that you can follow your ideas through and that you can do it.

No one is born with their instincts. Everyone learns them with time and so will you. But this happens when you are pursuing something with all your interest passion. When you become that much immersed in something, your mind will not require that much effort to draw knowledge from that subject. At that time, you will find that your instincts are no longer simply that but have become informed choices and they can be made in the blink of an eye.

If you find that rules are becoming the barrier in your path, then you should also know that you need not always follow the rules if your instinct is strong. The person who made those rules did so several years before you but if you want to be the leader now, you will be setting new rules with your instincts and that's the kind of thinking you have to develop.

Don't Make External Rewards Your Source of Motivation

It definitely feels good when you have all the nice things in life but are they enough to keep you motivated? The answer might seem to be yes as for now but it is never about prestige, money or any other such external rewards. Are you doing what you are doing for money or for gaining more power at the workplace? If the answer is yes, then your motivation level is sub-optimal. Whenever your motivation is based on something like this which is not really something that interests you or is a passion to you or it is based on feeling imposed, then your motivation will not last long.

You will never have the vitality or energy to accomplish your goals until and unless you do it because you love it. According to research, people might end up reaching their goals even with suboptimal motivation but in such cases, they cannot usually keep up with the effort in the long-term. When you are pushing your limits without having any healthy dose of motivation, you will not only be lagging behind but also face mental health issues. You will start procrastinating and getting out of bed every morning will start seeming like a very difficult task.

If you see someone who joins the gym, you will find that they visited the gym with so much enthusiasm on the first day. One the second day, their body will be sore but they still might be visiting although half-heartedly. And after that, irregularity will dawn and one day they will stop going to the gym totally. This is a very common story and this is exactly what happens in case of suboptimal motivation. If your only source of motivation is that you are going to shed some belly fat or gain those abs, then that motivation is not going to sustain you when your hands and legs turn sore. You need to be truly willing from the inside to hit the gym.

When you enjoy doing something intrinsically, it will never feel like you are putting any extra effort to do it. It will seem easy to you. You cannot rely on external sources of motivation forever. You will have to fall in love with the task itself to do it long-term.

Never Be Satisfied But Be Grateful

Before starting any discussion on this point, let me tell you one thing – I am not correlating not being satisfied with a state of unhappiness. You can easily ward off any unhappy feelings when you are grateful. But not being satisfied will help you push your limits and be unstoppable. When you are not satisfied, it means that it is not about the goal to you. Rather it is about the journey and the climb to reach that goal and all those things you learn along the way. The climb will open your eyes as to how much you can actually push yourself.

But even if you are showing this behavior, you need to stay grateful and humble because that is what will keep you grounded. Moreover, if you are able to hold on to this attitude, you will never get lazy or complacent. If you linger too much in your moment of success, you will become stagnant. So, you need to think about the next stop – the next goal. This is how you will keep walking towards better things with an unbeatable attitude.

But while you are doing all of this, you also have to be in control. Remember how I told you to act on your instinct. Well, that is exactly what you are going to do but never mistake it for impulse. Impulse and instinct are two completely different things.

Live Life on Your Own Terms

Never let society tell you what you should do or how you should do it. It is your decision and you should live life on our own terms. Build the confidence and self-respect you need to do what your heart is telling you to do. If you feel that there is something about your life that you don't feel to be right, then it is time that you take matters into your own hands and change it. People often think that the grass is greener on the other side. But in reality, someone from the other side of the fence will think that the grass is greener on your side. So, in short, the grass is green on both sides and you just have to realize it.

You also need to stay away from any of the toxic people that come into your life. Yes, they will try to point out mistakes and they will also try to make you unhappy but if you don't pay heed to what they say, you will not be affected by them as well. So, whenever you notice these negative people in your surroundings, you'll know that it is time for you to ditch them for your own good.

Also, you should never be holding yourself back. People do that for a variety of reasons. Sometimes they do it because they fear failure whereas sometimes they fear that others will judge them harshly. Whatever your fears are, you need to face them because they will only hold you back and do nothing else. When you are in a position that is difficult, you need to analyze it carefully and then act. Don't hold yourself back because if you do, only you will be the loser. Others will move past you and excel in life but you will remain where you are.

No matter what storm comes your way, you need to be confident about the fact that you can weather it. After all, you have made it this far, so why not more? When you start making decisions for your own good, you will feel good and you will truly start doing everything on your own terms without depending on others.

Don't Let Off the Pressure

It is true that some people don't perform well when they are under pressure but in some moments, the pressure is what keeps you going. Most people in this world can function when they are exposed to small doses of pressure but in the end, even they tend to relax by letting off the pressure. So, if you think you are truly passionate and unstoppable, you should be able to handle that pressure effectively without letting it hurt yourself. It will keep you active and alert but only if you let it to.

For this, you need to change your mindset. You cannot view pressure as something that is threatening. You need to see it as a fun challenge. Whenever you see a threat, your self-confidence will be undermined and you cannot let that happen. It can even lead to impulsive behavior. But if you try and shift your thoughts and see the pressure as a challenge, you will be doing way better. See the pressure-situation as an opportunity to push your limits and grow. Also, stop worrying about the outcome. You need to put all your focus on the task that you are currently doing.

When all your concentration is on doing great in the task and not wasting time thinking about the outcome, you will only be seeing the steps in front of you which serve as micro-goals. For example, consider a student who is writing his/her paper. If he/she concentrated fully on coming up with a stellar research, the paper will definitely turn out to be good but if the student wastes time thinking about what grades he/she is going to get, then all of that energy will be wasted for nothing.

You can also practice what-if situations. You can imagine the worst possible scenario that can happen and this, in turn, will help you prepare for the worst. So, even if the unexpected thing does happen, you will be ready to face it. So, in the hard times, you will not be losing your composure and you will have a contingency plan ready in your mind. Also, the task will not be compromised and you will be able to continue it with the best of your abilities.

When you will feel the pressure rising, there are certain things that might happen in such a situation. Anxiety can be one of them but you won't be able to control it. So, stop focusing on it. If you focus on something that you cannot control, the pressure will automatically get intensified. Focus on all those factors in front of you that you can control. You also need to believe in the good things and trust in yourself that you can bring a successful outcome. A person's strong sense of belief can take them to impossible places. When you act on confidence, all those feelings of fear and anxiety will be stripped off.

Don't Compete With Others

In today's world, you will often find others acting competitive with others in their vicinity. They often end up comparing their achievements and everything else with what others have done and this is not healthy. If you do this, you will end up staying stuck in an unending rat race. Yes, there will always be competition but you should not compete with others. The only person you should compete with is yourself. If you are in the habit of continuously checking what others are doing, then you need to stop it at once.

Chase your future self rather than competing with those around you. In most cases, the competitive nature of a person is often attached to ruthlessness but it shouldn't have been something like that. Instead, competitiveness should be correlated with betterment and ambition. But in some cases, you will come across people who have such a giving and team-oriented attitude and yet they are inherently competitive. What you have to do is that you have to strike a balance between being competitive and also being supportive to the same level. Only then can you funnel all your energy into doing something positive.

You need to run your own race. You will always find people in your life who reached the finishing point of some other race before you. For example, there will be someone who got married first just because you were busy growing your career. So, you need to stick to the race you are running and always look up to the greater scope of things. When you stop comparing yourself to others, you will face a relief because you no longer have to panic about others doing things ahead of you. You should know it in your heart that you will get what you want at the right time and the right place.

Also, when you stop comparing and competing with others, you will be able to open yourself up to the endless possibilities in this world. You will no longer have any boundaries to follow. There are so many things that you can pursue and when you see this, you will be immensely happy. The feeling that you get when you let go of what others expect you to do is incomparable and you will be happier than ever before.

Always Seek to Learn New Things

If you truly want to master what you do and be the best at it, you need to keep learning. You need to enhance your skillset and find newer ways in which you can improve your skills. You will always gain power from your unparalleled preparation. Every person who has made it big in this world never pretends to know everything because they understand the fact that there is always something new to learn. This is even truer now where technology is being upgraded with each passing minute.

Sometimes, you might feel frustrated to gain some new skill or learn something new. But no matter how tough the task is, the

74

happiness that you will get after completing is something that you cannot compare with anything else. Moreover, the more you learn, the more adapting you become and the person who knows how to adapt is the person who is most valuable to any team. Your mental toughness is not defined by how well you give solutions but by the fact that how well do you adapt to varying circumstances that come your way.

Also, you will never develop an arrogant attitude if you keep learning. No matter who you meet today, you will see that there is something to learn from everyone in life. Even if the person is not from your line of work or is completely different from you, there will always be something that seems fascinating and you can learn. When you keep learning, your professional creativity is boosted and you always have the freshest ideas. You will also be able to stay at par with this ever-changing world. Also, learning something new every day is also the best security tool that you can ever have.

No matter what path you have chosen in life, learning is an integral part of everything and you should never compromise it. With time, you will notice how expansive and big your mental library has become. Your passion is what drives you to work hard towards your goals. But sometimes this fire of passion might get weakened and that is why learning is important as it can keep fueling that fire. Research about some podcasts in your field and listen to them, follow mentors on social media, read books and other write-ups by your favorite leaders and you will keep learning new things.

Own Your Mistakes

We have already spoken about how failure is a prerequisite to success and you can learn a lot from it. But in between all of it, there is another thing that people often seem to forget. You have to own up to your mistakes too if you want to accept the failure. You can get stuck amidst some grave long-term implications if you do not learn to own your mistakes. When people don't own up to their mistakes, it usually leads to problems later on and it is something like adding fuel to a spark. The problem usually keeps expanding and gradually takes a form that you are not able to contain later on.

Also, when you point fingers at others when in reality it is you who has made the mistake, it shows a lack of integrity and it is something that a leader should not do. Have you thought what kind of an example you are setting for your team when you are putting blame on others for things of your own doing? You will not have a team if you keep behaving in such a manner. When you honestly start claiming your errors and show a proactive approach towards them, everyone will see you in a better light.

Moreover, when you own up to the mistake you have made, you will be building trust among your people. By committing a mistake, you might have affected the trust between your people but when you own your mistake, you are taking the first step towards rebuilding that trust. The overriding feeling of failure is one of the reasons why people don't accept their mistakes but when you finally admit that you have done something wrong, it takes a lot of courage to do it but you will feel happy and relieved.

When you keep suppressing small mistakes, they often tend to accumulate and cause larger problems but owning up to them will prevent any such thing from happening. If there is something that is highly detrimental to the health of your success then it is your act of using lies to cover up a mistake. So, if you want to solidify the genuineness of what you are doing and also develop a strong mental strength, you need to learn how you own your mistakes. And remember, your team members will shower you with grace if you accept that you have done something wrong but hiding the same will only give rise to judgmental behaviors and lack of trust.

Let Your Work Define You

Being a talker will not get you anywhere because talking is too shallow. But do you know what is deep? Your work. People will always remember what you have done and they will remember you for it. Boasting about your own work will never make you good in other people's eyes. Stop becoming that person who blows the trumpet of past achievements to whoever they meet. But this does not mean that I am telling you not to advertise your work. If you do not advertise your work, people will not magically come to know about the services you provide. So, what you need to do is to advertise your work but not yourself.

There will come a time when everyone will recognize you for your work and that is achieved through humbleness. If you keep boasting about how good you are then people will have quite the opposite impression of you and consider you as a shallow person. You need to keep improving your performance by working diligently day and night. Careful self-branding is the key to increasing your visibility and not self-boasting. It is true that the world is getting competitive with each passing day and in professional life, no one will wait for you but that doesn't mean you have to blow your own trumpet.

You need to be the go-getter. You need to create the impression that everyone can depend on you with full trust and that you will always be perfect at what you do. That is the person everyone prefers to work with. There is a fact that everyone seems to not see. People who are quiet about their efforts are the ones who surprise others with their great results. If you start bragging from the beginning that your results are going to be exemplary and somehow you fail to keep that mark, everyone will see you for the shallow person you are. But if you lay low and let your work do the talking, everyone will be amazed.

Keep Your Confidence Levels High

Confidence is the biggest asset anyone could possess. It is that attribute that cuts through everything be it economic status, age or beauty. It will instantly enhance your magnetism and also improve your work productivity. People who are confident in themselves do not get swayed by other's opinions of them. They do what they want to do irrespective of what others are saying or whether they are judging them or not.

People who are confident let their inner authority take charge of everything without worrying about what the consequences will be. But this doesn't make them arrogant or unethical. If someone is truly confident in a positive way, then they will know how to respect others and yet stay true to their instincts. Never be a people-pleaser. No good will come to you if you keep trying to be the right type of person or the person who wants to change themselves for others. No matter what the circumstance is, speak what you know to be the truth and not what others want you to say.

Another way to boost your confidence is not to be afraid to face your fears or back off when it comes to speaking about them.

Everyone has some soft underbellies and you should not be afraid to talk about them. If you try to hide your weaknesses within you, they will never be dealt with and they will always pull you back from feeling confident. There is nothing wrong with crying when you are in pain nor is it wrong to show others your authentic disappointments. This is all that makes you feel you. Displaying a pessimistic attitude towards everything in life is easy and everyone can do it. But being optimistic even in the hardest of times in the real deal and that is what confident people do.

Do not hide behind cynicism. You need to deal with everything head-on. You need to love yourself and you will become unstoppable because, after that, you will not have to depend on others for love. You do not have to rely on others to make you feel valuable. Know your self-worth and you will automatically feel confident.

Don't Carry Unnecessary Emotional Baggage

Your worst enemy on the road to success is those unnecessary kinds of stuff that are weighing you down. Everyone has some of them and you need to figure out how many unnecessary emotions you are having. Grab a pen and a piece of paper and write down all those thoughts and emotions you are having and you have to do this honestly. Once the list is done, you have to start your thinking process and figure out why you are having that particular thought and when exactly did you pick it up. Acknowledge all those painful moments of the past because acknowledging will make you strong. But remember, do not wallow in them.

One of the most common emotions that people carry around with them is guilt. Everyone makes mistakes and so will you. But that doesn't mean you have to carry that guilt all along your life. Humans tend to cling to guilt because they think they are punishing themselves in a way that they seem to be fit but this is not right. You are only hampering your own growth. You need to take a stand and stop this self-judgmental attitude. Don't indulge in the 'what if' games. One of the things that you can do to make yourself feel better is to seek forgiveness from those whom you have hurt or wronged and you will see how you can forgive yourself too.

Another emotional baggage present with almost everyone is regret. It is quite easy to fall prey to the thoughts where you say to yourself how good everything would have been in your life only if you had done things the other way around. But you need to keep in mind that the future is never in your hands and you cannot predict it. Stop playing the victim. You have made all those decisions yourself and some may be good and alternatively, some might turn out to be bad but that is just how it is. If you want to break free of any kind of negative emotion that is weighing you down, you first need to stop internalizing it.

Were you in a toxic relationship or are you still surrounded by people who make you sad? It can be anything. It might be someone who makes you feel abandoned, abused or it can also be unrequited love. You need to break free from all toxicity in your life only then can you truly be productive and happy. You also need to stop worrying about everything because most of the time, all those things you are worried about won't even matter in the long run. Carrying emotional baggage will only make you revisit past things that you have no control on and you will not be able to make any progress towards your goal.

Don't Complicate Things

It is very easy to become complicated even when everything in front of you is pretty simple. And the first step to do this is to improve your communication skills. Stop trying to read others' minds and take things simply. Bad communication is often the root of most problems in our life be it in the family or workplace. Another way in which things tend to become complicated is when we try to change people. You need to accept everyone for the way they are. Everyone is different and no one will fit exactly to your description of the perfect person. You need to be okay with this.

Save yourself from some stress that is completely needless. Give others some support and don't try to tell them what they should do. Procrastination is another reason why things become complicated. Make changes today and start taking some serious action. Don't leave everything for tomorrow. Practice discipline in your life because discipline is what will take you a long way into the future. When you constantly put something off for later, it becomes even more intense and scarier. If you don't start something today, you will never be able to finish it by tomorrow. So, the best time to start is now!

Also, you cannot satisfy everyone at the same time. Don't try to make everyone happy because that will make everything complicated for you. Promise yourself to make one person smile each day. Stop making promises when you know you cannot keep them because later on, you will drown in the feelings of guilt and shame. Under-promise but over-deliver. This should be the mantra of your life. Always keep track of the progress you have made. Being productive and being busy is not the same and you should understand that. Don't over commit and burn yourself out. Take the rest that you need and start with a fresh mind.

Set Aside Time For Rejuvenation

Are your goals taking away a lot of your creative and mental resources? It is quite common to see the goals of your life occupying the maximum part of your day and consuming all your energy. Yes, your goal might be your passion and you might love what you do but this doesn't mean that doing what you love won't cause any amount of fatigue or burnout. When you keep working constantly without taking any breaks, all your creative powers start diminishing. But if you want to improve your performance critically, you need to take some time out to reassess and rejuvenate.

Take a day off and don't let yourself work on anything during that time. When you take a day off, you will find yourself refocusing all your energy and gaining a lot of strength. There is no particular rule of getting a fixed amount of relaxation. It will differ from person to person. But what is important is incorporating a time of relaxation into your lifestyle and then enjoying and unwinding during that time. Also, when you are happy and doing things you love, the feel-good hormones are released and they can relieve you of all the stress and anxiety. You can also set aside a particular amount of time each day for exercise. It will not only keep you healthy but also give you a mental boost.

If you want to display effective leadership, then taking some time out of your daily routine to attend to your own mental health is necessary. When your mind is refreshed, you will be working with your energy levels at peak points and you will be making better decisions too. But when you are over-stretching your power to accommodate stress, there will come a point of time when you will snap. So, taking some 'me time' out of your busy schedule will give you the much-needed relaxation that will get you back on track and you will truly become unstoppable.

"The mind is everything. What you think you become." – Buddha

Chapter 6

How To Mentally Prepare For Challenges In Life, Career And Family?

Making changes in your lifestyle can go a long way in helping you prepare for all the challenges that come your way in your career, family or even life in general. Challenges might not always be external. Sometimes they are internal in the form of stress, anxiety, and depression. But the key to meeting any type of challenge is to be prepared for it. Yes, predicting the challenges is not always possible but you can arm yourself up for any possible bump on the road. Your current state of comfort is not permanent. There will be hard times and you cannot run away from them. If you want to lead a healthy life, you need to face your challenges and be mentally strong.

Here are some tips for you to prepare yourself mentally for any such challenges in life.

Don't Expect Success to Happen Overnight

You will often come across the term 'overnight success' in today's world but in reality, there is nothing like that. Everyone wants to hit their target overnight and become the new headline. There is always some author whose book becomes famous overnight or someone in the team who suddenly gets promoted a pretty higher rank and that definitely makes for a nice topic of chit-chat. But is it really what you see? No, you only see the gossip and the news.

There is so much hard work that the author has put into his/her book and when it reached the audience, it became a success. Similarly, the employee has been working so many extra hours for days after which his/her hard work got acknowledged. So, no one really sees all the things that go on behind the curtain. People don't hear all these things because these are not exciting. These are too commonplace. The person who had made it a hit now has worked for several days and months crafting that skill.

So, if you want to face the challenges in life, you cannot be demotivated by the fact that others are getting overnight success because there is nothing like that. Everyone has worked a lot before reaching that top tier. You need to start small and then you can make your way to the top and one day, make it big. You might have to sacrifice those fun weekend outings with your friends but you are not the only one doing it. Others are doing it as well. The only difference is that you are not seeing them doing it.

You also do not get to see the several setbacks and barriers the successful people have seen in their way. So, when things are not working out for you, just remember that your fight is no different from others'. Discipline and persistence are the two things that will take you a long way towards your goal. Set lofty goals and work hard. Stretch yourself, push your limits and give all in. You need to stay focused on your path. There will be days when you will not feel like doing anything but you have to get yourself up. Remind yourself that your dreams will not come true if you do not give the hard work that is required to fulfill those dreams.

Have a Community That Will Support You

Do you have a group of people where you brainstorm ideas together? This is a very healthy practice and if you do not have such a group, make one today. The presence of a community is always essential so that they can be there for you in times of need and they will be the ones you can look up to for support. Your community of people should be composed of those who genuinely care about your welfare. Life is tough and you never know when challenges come your way so having people who love you will keep you strong.

Put simply, when you have someone positive, someone who truly wants you to excel by your side, you will experience a feeling of comfort. This is because you will know that there is someone or some people who will provide you with their shoulder to cry on. These people will always try to uplift you even in the darkest times instead of others who try to push you down. Supporting you doesn't always necessarily have to mean to give you something material. It can be the simplest of things like listening to what you have to say or lightening up your mood.

People have this tendency where they end up absorbing the actions of the people they mix with. This makes forming your own community even more important. When you are with your own people, you know them. You have to form this community selectively and made up of people who will imbibe good values in you. When you are constantly around bright and impactful souls who are nothing but happy and supportive, you will automatically develop a similar attitude towards life. You will feel good about yourself and your goals will no longer seem unrealistic.

People you mix with can be quite impactful for your life. This is because along with the good people, some people act like parasites and they can suck all the good from you. When you form your own community, make sure the community is full of productive people and those with whom you can have healthy arguments. You will also get exposure to differing perspectives and if you can develop an attitude where you are ready to soak up knowledge then all these perspectives will ultimately help you in life when you are dealing with the challenges.

Always Believe That You Can Do It

Nor the resources neither the opportunity is what differs successful people from the unsuccessful ones. Rather it is the amount of self-belief that they have that makes a lot of difference. Your brain will play in several ways and most of the time against you even if you are doing everything else in the right way. And you need to understand this fact. Your brain will not care how big your goals are and so there arises an immense amount of self-doubt, procrastination, anxiety and negative thinking. But the only way in which you can get out of that toxic loop is to not believe in the negativities but in yourself.

And honestly, who do you think will believe in your abilities if you yourself don't? For example, think of a situation where you have some big idea which you are going to propose in front of the investors. Now, you need to impress the investors about the profitability and uniqueness of your idea. But will you be able to make a good case in front of them if you don't believe in your potential? No. Also, if you suffer from self-doubt, the person in front of you will see right through it and cancel your proposition then and there.

Life is not easy and everyone will keep judging and testing your competence in every matter until and unless you take a stand and believe in yourself. The amount of self-confidence you need cannot be bestowed upon you magically. It has to come from within and you need to start working upon it if you want to be successful. You have set your goals and you have also carved out the path to follow. Now, all you need is to walk upon that path with confidence. Accomplishing your goal will depend on your ability to trust yourself and this dependability is of huge proportions.

There will be countless obstacles and failures in your path and all of them will be temporary. You need to believe that maybe the next moment in your life is going to be pivotal and you have to be ready to give your best when it comes. Don't start finding excuses to avoid a certain situation. Doing that is extremely easy but working and battling the bumps on the road is what is hard and that will take you closer to your goals.

Your Goals Should Be Defined

Goal setting is so important and it should also be defined and not vague. If you don't know what your goals are, how are you going to feel motivated about them? One of the first ways in which goals can help you become unstoppable is that it helps triggering behavior. When your goals are specific, your behavior automatically becomes focused and actionable. In simpler terms, pure motivation arises from goal setting when done in the right way. For example, you want to save some money but you don't know how much, will that get you anywhere? No. But if you think that you want to save $5000 by the end of 6 months, then you have a specific goal and you can decide how much money you need to set aside each month for that lump sum to accumulate.

Moreover, when you have set a goal, you have a set of steps to follow. Thus, when you complete one step, you know that you have to move on to the next. It is like moving up a ladder and you also know the distance between each rung on the ladder. But you don't have your goals defined, you simply know that you have to climb but you don't know where the rungs are or how you should place your feet in order to climb them. In short, with defined goals, you get a direction in which you will start climbing.

But apart from the above-mentioned facts, one of the prime reasons why goal setting makes you more successful is because it helps you build your character. To be more precise, achieving success after following the steps to your defined goals is what builds your character. In the entire process of goal-setting, you will learn a lot of things, especially, what is important to you. You will unearth your inner self. But when you finally start pursuing your goals and building a mental strength to deal with everything come what may, this is what builds your self-efficacy.

If you trying to put off your goals until that some perfect day comes, then you need to stop doing it right now. Pushing your goals for some perfect future is never the solution. If you think that there will come a time when you will be ready, trust me, there is no such time. Every day is the perfect opportunity to start. All you need to do is seize it and take the first step no matter how daunting it is.

Be Dedicated

One of the primary reasons why a person becomes successful in life is because he/she was dedicated to their cause. If you have set your goals but are not committed to them, then you will never be able to achieve all that you want. The simplest meaning of dedication is to give something your complete focus and devotion. But don't misunderstand dedication as doing something forcefully. It means doing something with love. Although the primary component of the term is hard work, it should also be accompanied by love in order to yield the best results.

What most people don't want to discuss is how an unsatisfactory
life can hamper your success. But the direct road to satisfaction
is to pursue something you love and can do by staying dedicated
to it. But if you want to be dedicated to your work, first of all,
you need to come up with strategies that will truly help what you
are doing. For this, you have to spend a considerable portion of
your day brainstorming ideas and then analyzing whether or not
that idea will suit your circumstances. Also, you need to start
inspecting all the happenings in your daily life which means
both your professional and personal life. This will help you bring
things in order.

If you find anything in your life that is not following a smooth
course, you need to pick it up and then figure out what you can
do to make it better. You also need to do a proper analysis of the
big picture. You also need to maintain a balance between
everything. If you do not do that, then the stress levels will keep
increasing and meeting deadlines will become an even more
difficult task. But are you wondering how you will become
dedicative? Well, the first step is to make your healthy habits a
natural thing for you.

Do you think twice before brushing your teeth in the morning?
No, right? This is because you have been doing that for a long
time and you know that it is right for your personal hygiene.
Similarly, you have to practice healthy habits in other spheres of

life as well and when you continue doing them daily, they will occur naturally to you. And most, importantly, don't forget the small victories you are making because they will help you move forward.

Practice Journaling

Now, by journaling, I am not telling you to write every detail of your day. It is okay if you do that. But for others who are not a big fan of writing things down at the end of the day, you should at least try keeping a track of the progress you are making in a journal. Also, according to research, it has been proven that when people track their progress, they have a way higher tendency to reach their goals than those who don't. There is a very simple explanation for it as well. If you measure what you are doing, it creates a psychological effect and automatically pushes you to do more. For example, if you keep track of your expenses every month and see how much amount you have spent on food, you will automatically start saving.

Another important reason for tracking your progress is that it helps you understand your current standing. This, in turn, will gradually help you understand whether you are making progress or not. This process can also assist you in forming realistic goals. Let us consider this example. Suppose you have started gym and currently, you are doing 2,000 steps a day. Would it be realistic if you suddenly set the goal of 10,000 steps a day or would it be better to set it at 5,000? The latter, isn't it? That is what writing down your current standing does. It helps you figure what goals you should set in the first place.

Once you have figured out the baseline, keeping a track of every small thing that you are doing will help you mark your improvement. This will also promote you to celebrate your wins. No matter how small the achievement is, if you celebrate it, the achievement will become a lot bigger. This will keep you motivated. Thus, when you keep tracking what you are doing, you get a reason that urges you to celebrate with every small progress. And in this way, you will be taking baby steps towards your ultimate goal.

Also, if you keep a track of your progress right from the beginning, then you will also know when you have encountered a problem on the way. Or, even if you stop making progress, it will become prominent to you then and there. This will be possible only when you keep track right from the beginning.

Live a Positive Life

Filling your life with positivity and hope is the ultimate thing and this will put you on the path of becoming unstoppable. The first step to doing that is being happy with your lot. As already mentioned previously in this book, you need to stop comparing yourself to others. There will always be someone who has more

96

than what you have and that is completely okay. It is very easy to keep wishing for something else but you also need to remind yourself that when you are wishing for that other thing, someone else is wishing for what you have. So whatever you have, it might not seem enough to you but it is enough to someone else. In short, you should focus on what you have and how you can make it better instead of lamenting on what you don't have.

When you face the challenges in your life, you can either choose to run away from it or you can also choose to face them head-on. It is easy to stay stuck in a bad situation but you will have to gather the courage and mental strength to turn that bad situation into a good one and learn from it. Learn from the mistake that you have made and promise yourself that you are not going to repeat it. That is how an unstoppable person should behave. You should keep walking irrespective of the storm around you.

The thing that makes you feel secure is also the thing that brings negativity into your life and that is the need to control. When you have everything in your control, you feel secure but the moment something happens out of line, you feel that you have lost it all. But you should keep you calm, analyze the situation for the way it is without exaggerating any of the details and then come up with a realistic solution. The more you try to have control over every aspect of your life, the more panicky you will become.

You also need to let go of the resentment inside of you, if any. If you are in pain or if you are angry, you need to speak about it and resolve the issues. Bottling them up will only hamper your productivity. You can either speak about your feelings to someone close to you, maybe your family, or you can also seek the help of a mentor.

"Our ability to handle life's challenges is a measure of our strength of character." – Les Brown

Chapter 7

Correlation Between Mental Toughness And Physical Toughness

Often considered as an important necessity of a successful life, is mental toughness any different from physical toughness? Well, if you ask those around you, most of them will say no. But if you think clearly, you will realize that there isn't that much difference between these two things. When you try to develop physical toughness, you also need to be tough mentally. But for some reason, people consider them differently. But no matter what type of success you are speaking about, all of it has its origin in one single place, and that is your mind.

As I have mentioned time and again, persistence is the key to developing toughness. Anyone who has the habit of constantly quitting their endeavors is not someone who will acquire mental toughness. One of the best ways to develop this sense of toughness is when you start working out. In the first few days, you are going to have a hard time. But do you quit? No. You keep working hard. You tell yourself that you are going to do one more rep and that might take all your physical effort, but it will ultimately make you physically and mentally strong. When you push your limits and endure the pain, the sense of becoming tougher will start settling in because you have just broken a boundary.

When you go out in the morning and tell yourself that you are going to run for 5 km today, complete the run. Do not listen to that voice in your head which constantly keeps telling you that you can try it the next day and you can take a break. No, the happiness that you will get once you complete the run is nothing compared to that momentary relief you get in a break or by postponing the run for the next day.

The same level of mental toughness can also be developed when you are at work. For example, there are days when you have to stick to your desk for hours meeting deadlines. It is pathetic and you will also be in a constant war with your mind which will keep telling you to simply keep all the work and go home. What will you do? Will you fall weak and let your inner voice win? Or will you fight it and continue your work until your scheduled rest period? I think you should go with the latter if you want to build mental toughness. But do you see how physical toughness is involved here? You are working for long hours and that is strenuous. So, you have to gather all the energy you have and focus on the task at hand. This involves building your physical toughness.

There will be times when your mind will wander off to places and that will make it tougher for you to concentrate but you will have to stay strong. The moment you complete the task, you will feel victorious. It might seem a small victory to you at the moment, but you need to celebrate it because it will make you feel better about your character and your integrity to your goals.

Toughness and discipline come hand in hand. If you are not disciplined in the course of your life, you will never be able to be tough. Another thing that you need to get straight is that toughness is about your habits. Motivation might keep you going but at the end of the day, even motivation is a fickle concept and you cannot afford to be fickle with something that you are serious about. So, when you start building your daily habits, you have to work physically to develop your mental toughness. For example, if you want to wake up at a certain time in the morning each day, you will have to push yourself to do that. This means you have to bring about your sense of physical toughness which again arises from mental toughness that you are determined about doing a certain thing.

If you think that people who are mentally tough, had to be more intelligent or talented to become the way they are, then you are wrong. All they had to do was be consistent. When you are successful at becoming mentally tough, you learn how to focus everything on one particular goal. And, you will stick to your path no matter how many obstacles try to stop you. That is a true example of consistency. You will be overcoming all the problems over and over again. And in order to do this, you have to have the right mindset which is strong.

You do not have to start with life-changing transformations. Start with small things. Don't let your dreams drive you into a frenzy. Be cool-headed and figure out the micro-goals that will lead you up to your ultimate goal in life. You need to start small. No matter how big your dreams are, they are achievable and don't let anyone tell you otherwise. But all you need to do is take small steps instead of taking bigger leaps. Did you ever find a child in your life who learned how to run before they learn walking? No, right? Because that is not how things happen. You have to take the beginner's lessons before you can move on to the expert ones.

Now, this doesn't mean that you won't slip. You will. But the ultimate aim is to pick yourself up. That is what a mentally and physically strong person would do. Don't let the small hiccups in your path affect your dream goal. Your motivation and willpower and consistency are what make you different from a person who is not so mentally tough. No matter how small your changes are, every change is significant and so is every win. It is okay if you cannot keep up with the optimal schedule. Just give your best and you will see results.

So, the next time anyone tells you that mental and physical toughness are two different things, you know that they aren't.

"My strength did not come from lifting weights. My strength came from lifting myself up when I was knocked down." – Bob Moore

Chapter 8

7 Effective Ways To Be Strong In Every Situation

In life, staying mentally acute is very important. You will always have to make some tough decisions and staying mentally strong is what will take you forward. You can sometimes even get complex information that you have to process in order to move past a situation. If you want to make the right decisions at the right time, you have to remain sharp. So, you will have to do a lot of things at a time. You will have to manage all your emotions and you will also have to shove aside all those negative thoughts and choose the positive ones. In short, you have to adjust your thinking to suit the circumstances. But mental strength will not come to you in a day and you have to build it. So no matter what situation comes in your life, here are seven ways that will help you stay strong.

Focus On The Moment

You will face challenges in your path from time to time and all of them are basically a test to see how you deal with them. Whether you are willing to make a change and stretch your boundaries is all that will matter. But, the worst thing to do would be ignoring the situation altogether or procrastinating. You need to develop solutions for the challenges if you want to deal with them the right way. You need to remember that your difficulty has to be dealt with right now as your challenge is also in the present tense. You need to focus on your present and not worry about any other things.

If you think about your future or your past, you might lose all that is in front of you and also lose yourself to the challenge. Your present is where life unfolds itself but it is the natural tendency of people to let it all slip away. People do not observe things while they are passing by and lament on the loss later on. The most common trait seen among people today is that they love to fantasize. When they are busy with deadlines knocking on their door, they love to think about the next vacation but when they are on vacation, they start thinking about all those new proposals they are going to make back at the office. So, you are never really dealing with your present.

So, you need to aware of your present if you want to deal with all kinds of situations in your life. And not only this, but you also have to build a non-judgmental outlook for everything. But don't think that I am against planning. Strictly no, because that would be misguidance. Plan, but don't lose sight of what is happening now. You also got to remember that no matter how much planning and goal-setting you do, what you can really control is your present and so amidst all of this, don't forget where you are.

Also, when you think too much about what is going to happen, you start accumulating stress. This can prove to be detrimental to your overall well-being. You need to learn to invigorate your life with strategies that will actually come of help to you in your present. It is a well-known fact that if you want to be happy, it is your present that you need to focus on and being happy will clear your mind so that you can deal with all those things that come as obstacles.

Remember That Everything is Temporary

Have you ever seen rains all around the year? Have you ever seen an earthquake continue for an endless amount of time? No, right? It is because nothing is permanent in this world. They are all just passing phases and will end in a certain amount of time. When you get hurt, it will keep bothering you and even affect you for days, months or sometimes even a year. But after that, you will start healing or you will get used to it. Those pangs you felt in the initial days will subside and the pain will start becoming bearable and eventually, you will be seeing the happy days. This is something you need to remind yourself when you are low.

You will always notice elders telling you the age-old saying that there is always light after darkness and this is one hundred percent true. No dark period of your life will last forever so there is no need for you to completely break down over it. So, if you are seeing that things are good now, you need to enjoy but if things take a different turn, there is no end to think that is the end of the world because it is not. If your life is not currently on the easy road, you do not need to worry yourself to depression that it is not going to be okay ever. This exact thinking is what will make your challenges worse.

You need to embrace the adversity that comes your way by reminding yourself that it will not last long. It is simply a passing phase meant to test the skills you have acquired so far. You need to see these challenges as stepping stones of your life. Facing challenges is not a dead end. Alternatively, when you face difficult situations, you also end up learning something new from that exact situation.

Push Yourself to Take the Next Step

Pure perseverance doesn't come in a day but it is also a quality that makes up a leader and someone who is successful in life. This becomes even more important in today's world where the culture has taken a turn towards wanting quick results. There is beauty in putting all your effort into something and waiting patiently for the results. All you need to do is identify that beauty and embrace it as your own. Be present, strong and steadfast.

You must have heard it a million times by now but I am reiterating it once again. The most beautiful smile is the one that has gone through all the trouble and still standing strong after shedding all those tears. You know why? Breakthroughs come to those who have already faced a million breakdowns. There is a solution contained in every heartbreak that you have gone through or every failure that has come your way. The lesson might be subtle but it is there waiting to be recognized so that you do not repeat your mistakes and fall prey in the same way again.

So, if you are in search of the most reliable future prediction then I can give you one advice. There is no such thing as that. If you want to be certain about your future, you need to be able to create it yourself. If you do not participate in your present life, you will simply have to wait and watch while it passes you by. You will simply be a silent observer. There are only a few things in life that you do not have any control over. If you keep obsessing over those same things then you will be losing all those many things in life which you can actually control.

There will come a time in everyone's life when they will have to face failure. But in that moment of failure, you need to remind yourself, your failure is not what defines you but how you deal with it does. The more failure you get in life, the wiser you will be because each of these failures will teach you something or the other. You need to keep pressing on and you will get what you are looking for. Simply waiting for good things in life won't bring you anything. You definitely have to be patient but you also have to work hard to make those good things happen. And for that, you need to push your limits and walk those extra miles when no one else is seeing so that you can rise and shine one day. It is about bringing up the courage to stand up even in the face of adversity. Yes, you will be scared but the test is to see whether you take the step anyway.

Don't Let Your Negativity Take Over You

You need to maintain a positive attitude every day. You might be thinking that there is not really any particular reason for you to be happy but you have to be and you have to push all negative feelings outside. Being positive is not a response. If you want to achieve success, you need to consider being positive as a strategy. It is a strategy that will bring you closer to your ultimate goal. Do you when is the most powerful and essential time for you to practice being positive? It is exactly when everything around you is not so much positive. That is when you need to put in all your effort and create a positive mindset.

Do you feel jealous when you see others happy? Well, no one handed the happiness over to them. They are happy because they chose to be happy and they did not allow their negative feelings to take over them. You, on the other hand, can be happy too but only if you plan to do so. When people are happy, it does not mean that they got any fewer amounts of problems in their life. It simply means that they know how to compartmentalize their issues and not let the bad things take over. In simpler terms, the absence of problems is not what happiness is. It is an inner state of mind.

You need to raise your awareness of positivity. You need to identify what your inner strength is otherwise your daily challenges will always keep winning and you will always keep losing. How you are reacting to the events of your life is completely your decision and in your hands. Whether or not you let negativity take over the good things in your life is also your decision. So, be grateful and appreciate all that you have because some people don't even have that.

There should be no reason for you to be positive and you shouldn't be waiting for one. Being positive is something that should come naturally to you. Choose positivity at every moment. Look up to the numerous possibilities you have in your life. No matter how hard life becomes, you always have yourself and you need to look forward from there and not back. You need to figure out ways to make your positive vision empowered. Your outcomes are created by you and that happens when you are able to resonate with the vision you are creating.

Don't Try to Conquer Everything at Once

We have spoken about goal setting several times in this book but one thing that you need to understand if you want to make things simpler is that no one has asked you to start conquering mountains. Make goals that are realistic. If instant gratification is what you are seeking, then you are going to have a hard time in your life. Sometimes, you might even feel frustrated or painful. Life is made up of so many tiny moments. Make each moment worthwhile. Promise to yourself that you are going to take small steps in every moment to do something for your welfare. You are going to make small investments for your betterment. And then, you will see the rewards coming to you naturally.

There will be so many things in your life that you might think needs fixing. This becomes even truer when everything in your life is taking a wrong turn. In such situations, no matter how fundamental your effort is, it can make a whole world of difference to your life. Great opportunities can arise in situations of great adversity but all you have to do is keep your eyes and ears open. You can create a lot of value when everything all around you is going wrong.

Complacency is something that can lull you into its clutches when you are going through a good phase in your life. In those times, you might even forget your true worth or how resourceful you can be when time demands. But you can indulge in perseverance if you promise yourself about doing something little every day. These minor fixes, when repeated on a daily basis, will be small steps and one day you will be far ahead from where you are today. Isn't that quite a progress and way better than staying stagnant?

Tiny fixes are all you need and they can get you out of any kind of trouble you are in. But on the other hand, when you try to do everything at once or try to climb mountains, you can easily get overwhelmed and end up making the wrong decisions. Also, when you take these small steps and eventually see good things happening around, you will feel more motivated and this will go on like a positive cycle of growth. So, what are you waiting for? Start today and reap your results later.

Appreciate Even the Small Things in Life

People often complain that they do not have enough to appreciate so why should they be grateful. Do you think this is true? Well, I don't. Do you want to know why? Here's why. You might be thinking that there is not much to be grateful for because you do not have what you want. Well, who does? The world is not Aladdin's genie that they will keep granting you wishes. You have to make it happen if you really want something. You have to work hard to achieve what you want. But, in the meantime, think about the smallest things in life. You may have been cheated, hurt or even betrayed by your closest people but you still do have a lot of things to appreciate because there will always be someone who doesn't have what you have.

Have you ever thought about it this way? Go back a decade and think about what you wanted then. I'm sure you have some of those things. So, while you are lamenting about what you don't have, you forget to appreciate the fact that you have things which you could only dream of ten years back. Isn't that an achievement? I would definitely call it that. And that is exactly why you need to be appreciative of life. Don't waste away your time thinking about your failures or what you don't have.

Do you think it is naïve that some people stay positive even when everything around them is screaming of negative things? No, it is not because that is how leadership should look like. If you, as a leader, give in to negativity, what would your team do? How will they work hard to achieve results when their leader has surrendered to some mere obstacles on the path? Life might be giving you a lot to complain about but you still have to put on your best face and smile.

What if you woke up tomorrow and find that all of that you were not thankful for has been taken away from you? Will you feel good? That is exactly why you need to be thankful for literally everything including the most ordinary things which are, in reality, not so ordinary. The moment you start showing appreciation for what you have, you will feel good and happy. This will also give you a boost when you are facing new challenges. This will keep you going even in the most adverse situations.

Love Yourself

When you start ignoring your own emotions or what your mind is telling you about your mental health, it usually takes a toll on your productivity and mental strength. So, don't ever let that happen. Pay heed to all those signs you are getting about a possible burnout or anxiety attacks. Take a day off and pamper yourself. Do what makes you relieved. Developing a state of mind where you are constantly facing stress, anxiety or depression is extremely unhealthy and you need to take a step to stop that from happening.

All of this usually results from self-neglect, which, let's be honest, most of us do. When we have deadlines looming over our heads, do we think about the fact that we have been stretching our work hours consistently for days? Do we think twice before taking on a big proposal even though we have lots on our plate? The answer to both of these questions is no and that is exactly what you need to stop. When you go too deep into the habit of self-neglect, it can become a part of you and then it will be quite difficult to break out from that cycle. So, the moment you start to notice yourself ignoring your health, you need to nip the habit in the bud.

It is quite common for people to spend more than half of their lives trying to shrink themselves in all manners possible. People try to become less opinionated. They try to become less needy. They try even harder to become less sensitive. But in all these things, they also become less of them. They lose their own personality to the flow of life and this is something you need to prevent. You don't have to fit in. Be you. If someone truly wants to be a part of your life, then they will learn to adjust. You don't have to do everything so that you can please the other person. All you have to do is please yourself and everything will be fine. Don't sacrifice all that you hold dear just for the sake of making others form a good impression of you. You don't have to fit into the idea of a worthwhile person and shrink yourself just because someone else wants you to. You are already the best and you need to love yourself for who you are.

"Stay strong. Stand up. Have a voice." – Shawn Johnson

Conclusion

Thank you for making it through to the end of *Mental Toughness: The Ultimate Guide To Train Your Brain, Boost Your Resilience, Discover How To Be Relentless With True Mindset And Become Unbeatable With An Unstoppable Mind*, let's hope it was informative and able to provide you with all of the tools you need to achieve your goals whatever they may be.

The next step is to use the knowledge acquired to develop your mental toughness. I'm not saying that you are inherently mentally weak. Everyone possessed some amount of mental strength but there will always be room for improvement. When you browse the web, you will find that there is a lot of misinformation about mental toughness but this book has been written from both extensive research and personal experience to give you a comprehensive set of knowledge on the subject.

But you shouldn't be of the impression that acting tough from the outside is what mental toughness is about because it is nothing like that. You do not need to suppress all your emotions in order to be mentally tough and this book will teach you how you can actually become a mentally strong person. You might be mentally strong when everything in your life is going on the right path but when something goes wrong, that is when the real test starts. I hope you start dealing with situations in a different way now that you have read the book and I hope you will have a more content life.

Finally, if you found this book useful in any way, a review on Amazon is always appreciated!